Original title:
True Friends: Recognizing Authentic Connections

Copyright © 2024 Swan Charm
All rights reserved.

Author: Sabrina Sarvik
ISBN HARDBACK: 978-9916-89-073-8
ISBN PAPERBACK: 978-9916-89-074-5
ISBN EBOOK: 978-9916-89-075-2

Lanterns in the Dark

In the still of night, they glow,
Whispers of hope softly flow.
Casting light on paths unseen,
Guiding dreams where hearts have been.

Flickering flames in gentle breeze,
Filling shadows with warm ease.
Each lantern a story told,
Of love and courage bold.

Beneath the stars, they sway and dance,
Inviting souls for a second chance.
In the silence, they ignite,
A spark of joy, a beacon bright.

Through the gloom, they shine their way,
Offering comfort, come what may.
With every flicker, they impart,
The simple truths that fill the heart.

Lanterns flicker, souls renew,
Embracing darkness, finding you.
Together, we'll light up the night,
With lanterns guiding our shared light.

Melodies of the Heart

Softly strumming gentle chords,
Echoing love in whispered words.
Each note a dream that takes its flight,
Melodies weaving through the night.

Rhythms pulse like beating hearts,
Binding souls with delicate arts.
In harmony, we find our way,
Creating magic day by day.

Every song a tale to tell,
Of laughter, joy, and times we fell.
In the silence, music grows,
A tapestry of highs and lows.

Notes entwine like vines that climb,
Crafting moments frozen in time.
With every beat, each breath we find,
Melodies connect both heart and mind.

In this rhythm, we are free,
Sharing melodies, you and me.
Together, we'll write our part,
In the symphony of the heart.

The Essence of Loyalty

In shadowed paths we walk together,
Bound by promises, light as a feather.
Through storms and trials, hand in hand,
A silent vow, a steadfast stand.

Your spirit whispers, strong and true,
In darkest hours, I cling to you.
Each heartbeat echoes, love lush and bright,
In loyalty's embrace, we find our light.

Roots Entwined

Deep beneath the earth we grow,
Our roots entangled, hearts aglow.
In storms that shake, we hold our ground,
A bond unbroken, love profound.

Through seasons change, we shift and sway,
Yet in our core, we choose to stay.
Nurtured by trust, we reach for the sky,
Together we flourish, you and I.

Echoes of Trust

In whispers soft, our secrets dwell,
A sacred promise, a comforting swell.
With every glance, understanding grows,
In the silence shared, true friendship flows.

Through laughter bright and tears so warm,
We weather life's unpredictable storm.
In every heartbeat, our stories weave,
Echoes of trust, forever believe.

Unseen Ties

Invisible threads connect our souls,
Binding us gently, making us whole.
In moments quiet, your presence stays,
Guiding me softly through life's maze.

With every challenge, we rise anew,
These unseen ties, holding me to you.
In the dance of life, we find our grace,
In the warmth of friendship, a sacred space.

Illuminated Pathways

Soft whispers guide the way,
With every step, we sway.
In shadows, light does dance,
A chance for every glance.

Stars above, a gentle glow,
The journey teaches so.
With courage, hearts ignite,
Together, we take flight.

In the night, dreams arise,
Illuminating skies.
Paths unfold like dreams,
Life is more than it seems.

Nature sings, a song so sweet,
With every heart, we meet.
Through darkness, we believe,
In love, we all achieve.

Embracing every turn,
With patience, we will learn.
A tapestry of grace,
Guiding us through this space.

Gems of Affection

In shadows, kindness gleams,
Woven through our dreams.
Every smile a treasure,
Moments without measure.

Words like diamonds shine bright,
In darkness, they bring light.
Hearts entwined so closely,
In love, we dance mostly.

Within laughter, joy blooms,
Through sorrow, it consumes.
Life's sweetest embrace,
In our shared space.

Friendship's warmth, a fire,
Fueling every desire.
Gems of trust we create,
In every heart, we cultivate.

Time unfurls like a scroll,
In every heart, a soul.
Together, we are strong,
In the light, we belong.

The Circle of Trust

Within a ring, we stand tall,
Bound by love, we won't fall.
Voices unite in song,
In trust, we all belong.

Hands held tight, fears subside,
With you, I can confide.
In laughter, we find peace,
In silence, sweet release.

Through storms that may arise,
We gaze into each other's eyes.
A bond that will not break,
In every step we take.

Secrets shared, gently kept,
In moments, love adept.
A treasure more than gold,
Together, brave and bold.

As seasons shift and turn,
From each other, we learn.
In this circle, we find,
A safe place for the mind.

Stories Shared

In the flicker of the flame,
Tales of life, never the same.
Words weave through the night,
In shadows, shared delight.

Memories painted bright,
In laughter, pure light.
In stories, hearts embrace,
A journey through time and space.

With every whispered word,
A connection unheard.
Ears open, hearts aligned,
In shared tales, love defined.

Pages turn with each breath,
In every story, life and death.
Together, we explore,
In narratives, minds soar.

The tapestry of voices,
In each, a heart rejoices.
In the quiet and the loud,
In stories, we are proud.

Unwavering Presence

In the quiet of the night, we stand,
Two souls, a bond that's boldly planned.
Whispers dance on the gentle air,
Together in moments, we lay bare.

Through storms that threaten to break our way,
Your strength holds me, come what may.
In shadows cast, in light that gleams,
We walk hand in hand, chasing dreams.

With every laugh and tear we share,
In each heartbeat, you show you care.
An anchor in the tide of doubt,
In you, my love, I have no drought.

Time may fade, but not our spark,
In every whisper, we'll leave a mark.
Unwavering, this promise we make,
Together always, for love's sweet sake.

So here within this sacred space,
Our journey blooms with every trace.
Forevermore, side by side,
In the depths of love, we confide.

The Canvas of Companionship

Upon the canvas, colors blend,
Each brushstroke tells of love unpenned.
Shades of laughter, hues of trust,
In every layer, we find our gust.

Together we paint, with heart and soul,
Creating a masterpiece, whole and bold.
Every moment, a vibrant hue,
In the art of us, forever true.

Through strokes of joy and shades of pain,
Our canvas grows, sun and rain.
With tender hands, we shape our fate,
In every corner, we celebrate.

Each texture speaks of days gone by,
Of dreams we caught beneath the sky.
With vibrant spirit, in unity,
We craft our tale, our symphony.

In the gallery of time, we stay,
Each moment carved in bright display.
Together we'll frame this love's embrace,
On the canvas of life, our sacred space.

Genuine Reflections

In mirrors clear, our truths unfold,
The warmth of love, a story told.
Honest eyes, a soft parade,
In genuine light, our fears allayed.

Here we stand, stripped of disguise,
Each glance reveals, no need for lies.
With open hearts, we delve so deep,
In the silence, secrets seep.

We share our dreams, both big and small,
In each other's gaze, we find it all.
With gentle words, our souls converse,
In genuine reflections, we immerse.

Through trials faced, our spirits grow,
In every doubt, we learn to flow.
Together we mend, together we rise,
In love's pure light, we realize.

So let us cherish this sacred bond,
In genuine moments, we respond.
With every heartbeat, our truth stays clear,
An unwavering love, forever near.

Sincere Embrace

In tender moments, arms entwined,
A safe haven, two hearts aligned.
With warmth that wraps like summer's day,
In sincere embrace, we find our way.

Each hug a fortress, strong and true,
In every pause, I'm close to you.
With whispered words that softly flow,
In love's embrace, we freely grow.

Through storms and trials, hand in hand,
In the stillness, we understand.
With every heartbeat, love's gentle trace,
In the comfort of a sincere place.

As shadows fade, and sunlight streams,
We find our strength in shared dreams.
In open arms, we heal, we mend,
In sincere embrace, we shall ascend.

Let these moments forever stay,
In the warmth of love, come what may.
In our together, we will face,
The world anew, in sincere grace.

An Unbreakable Bond

In times of joy, in times of pain,
Together we dance, together we stain.
With every laugh, with every tear,
We weave a story, deep and clear.

Through storms we weather, through nights so long,
Side by side, we grow more strong.
Hand in hand, we'll face the fight,
In the darkest hour, you are my light.

The echoes of laughter, the comfort of touch,
In the silence, your presence means so much.
In every heartbeat, in every sigh,
An unbreakable bond that will never die.

Through distance and time, we remain close,
A treasure more precious than any rose.
In the tapestry of life, our colors blend,
In this journey of love, there's no end.

So here we stand, united in grace,
In the story of us, every shadowed place.
Forever together, in heart and mind,
An unbreakable bond, forever entwined.

Whispers in the Wind

Gentle whispers ride the breeze,
Carrying secrets through the trees.
Stories of ages, tales untold,
In every rustle, mysteries unfold.

The soft caress of nature's breath,
Reminds us all of life and death.
In moments quiet, we start to hear,
The whispers calling, so crystal clear.

Beneath the stars, beneath the moon,
Nature's melodies form a tune.
In the shadows, in the light,
Whispers weave through the fabric of night.

When life gets heavy, when paths grow dim,
Listen closely, the wind sings a hymn.
A reminder that all will be well,
In their whispers, our hearts swell.

So close your eyes, embrace the flow,
Let the whispers guide you, let them show.
In timeless echoes, we may find,
Joyful solace in whispers of wind.

The Unbreakable Thread

A thread of gold, so finely spun,
Connecting souls, two become one.
Through trials faced, through dreams we chase,
This unbreakable thread, we embrace.

In laughter shared, in sorrows borne,
The fabric of life is beautifully worn.
With every stitch, our stories blend,
In this tapestry, there is no end.

Miles apart, yet always near,
In the silence, we can hear.
A heartbeat's rhythm, a pulse so true,
This thread of ours, binds me to you.

Through seasons change, through skies so gray,
This woven bond will never fray.
Each moment cherished, each memory fed,
Life's journey blessed by this thread.

So take my hand, and hold it tight,
Together we'll dance through day and night.
For in our hearts, forever fed,
Is the love sewn by the unbreakable thread.

Souls in Harmony

Two souls dance in synchrony,
Melodies of love set free.
In every glance, a spark ignites,
In every touch, the world feels right.

Through trials faced, through laughter loud,
In every heartbeat, we're both proud.
In quiet moments, together we breathe,
In this embrace, our souls believe.

From dawn's first light to midnight's hue,
In the vast expanse, it's me and you.
Through storms that rage and winds that howl,
In our rhythm, we both growl.

The universe spins, yet we hold tight,
In the symphony of stars at night.
With every note, every grace we share,
Souls in harmony, beyond compare.

So let this bond forever grow,
In this dance of life, let love flow.
For in our hearts, a song's decree,
Two souls entwined, in harmony.

When Eyes Speak

In silence deep, our gazes meet,
A language formed, so pure, so sweet.
No words are needed, just a glance,
In those bright pools, we find our chance.

Each flicker tells of joy and fear,
A whispered truth we hold so near.
They dance with warmth, a gentle spark,
Illuminating shadows dark.

When laughter shines, they brightly glow,
In sorrow's grip, they gently flow.
The stories tucked within their seams,
Are woven threads of hopes and dreams.

With every blink, a tale unfolds,
In every tear, a secret holds.
Together bound, our hearts in sync,
In this pure silence, we both think.

The Heartfelt Chorus

In harmony, our voices rise,
A symphony beneath the skies.
With every note, emotions soar,
A connection felt, forevermore.

Through laughter's highs and sorrow's lows,
The heartbeat of our story flows.
Each whisper shared creates a line,
A melody, your heart with mine.

In gentle chords, our dreams entwine,
Creating paths where stars align.
Like rivers merge to form a sea,
Our heartfelt chorus sets us free.

Together strong, we brave the night,
With harmony, we seek the light.
In every rise, in every fall,
Our song resounds, it binds us all.

Authentic Echoes

In every laugh, the truth conveyed,
In whispered thoughts, connections laid.
A resonance that's deep and clear,
Authentic echoes, always near.

Through trails we paved, in steps we take,
The stories shared, the bonds we make.
In moments fleeting, we find our way,
In echoes past, we choose to stay.

With every heartbeat, stories blend,
In every trial, we find a friend.
Our voices blend in gentle flow,
Authentic echoes, always glow.

Beneath the stars, our truths collide,
In every pulse, we will reside.
So here we stand, hand in hand,
In the echoes, we understand.

Pathways of Understanding

In each encounter, bridges build,
With every heart, our dreams are filled.
Through whispered thoughts and open minds,
On pathways where true love reminds.

With every step, we learn to see,
The different shades of you and me.
In every story shared, we find,
The threads that weave our lives aligned.

Through trials faced and victories grand,
We take the time to understand.
With kindness, patience, hearts entwined,
Creating pathways, love defined.

In every glance, a world revealed,
In every sigh, our hearts are healed.
Together we'll explore, embrace,
On pathways of understanding, our place.

Seeds of Loyalty

In gardens where our trust does grow,
We plant the seeds, with care we sow.
Through storms and sun, we stand as one,
A bond of loyalty, never undone.

With roots entwined, we rise so high,
Facing the winds, we will not die.
Together we flourish, strong, and free,
In the embrace of unity, you and me.

Each promise made, a blossom bright,
In darkest hours, we find our light.
With every challenge, our roots grow deep,
In loyalty's arms, our hopes we keep.

Through trials faced, we find our way,
With steadfast hearts, we seize the day.
In every season, through joy and strife,
The seeds of loyalty give us life.

When Laughter Heals

In moments shared, a laughter breaks,
A simple joy, a light that wakes.
The heaviness lifts, burdens unwind,
In giggles and grins, solace we find.

A gentle chuckle, a warm embrace,
In shared delight, we find our place.
The music of laughter, a healing tune,
Together we dance, beneath the moon.

In joyful echoes, pain starts to fade,
With every smile, new hopes are laid.
Through trials endured, our spirits rise,
In the heart of laughter, the healing lies.

Let worries drift like leaves in the breeze,
A shared moment, our minds at ease.
In the laughter lived, our joys conceal,
A gentle reminder, when laughter heals.

The Embrace of Understanding

In silence shared, a glance, a nod,
In the depths of hearts, a path we trod.
With every word, we bridge the gap,
In the embrace of understanding, we map.

Through stories told, we find our way,
In shades of empathy, love's array.
Two souls entwined, in gentle grace,
In the warmth of trust, we find our place.

When shadows loom, and doubts arise,
In understanding's glow, truth never lies.
With open hearts, we see the light,
Together we journey, day or night.

In every tear, in every cheer,
The bond we share is perfectly clear.
In the embrace of understanding, we stand,
Hand in hand, we'll explore this land.

Silent Echoes

In whispered thoughts, the silence sings,
A world of secrets, the heart brings.
In quiet moments, we learn to see,
The silent echoes that set us free.

Beneath the surface, emotions flow,
In stillness, truths begin to grow.
With every heartbeat, a story saves,
Amongst the shadows, the silence paves.

In the twilight dance, the whispers play,
In tranquil dreams, our fears decay.
The echoes linger, soft and clear,
In silent moments, we find no fear.

In the quiet dawn, a promise stays,
As silent echoes weave through the haze.
With every breath, we learn to trust,
In the depth of silence, it's all a must.

Ties that Transcend

Through shadows deep and whispers light,
We find a bond that feels just right.
What keeps us close, beyond all fear,
Are threads of love that persevere.

In laughter shared, in tears we send,
This journey long, with hearts to mend.
Each moment cherished, day by day,
In timeless dance, we find our way.

Against the tide, we stand as one,
With dreams ignited, never done.
In every heartbeat, every breath,
Our ties remain, defying death.

Though distance stretches, seas may roam,
Our spirits soar, we're never alone.
In quiet nights or sunlit morns,
The ties we weave can never be torn.

Through thick and thin, we shall endure,
With open hearts, our love is pure.
In every moment, hand in hand,
Our lives entwined, forever planned.

The Aroma of Shared Memories

In kitchens warm, where laughter bubbles,
Familiar scents, a dance of troubles.
Each recipe holds stories untold,
An essence cherished, a love bold.

From morning brews to evening feasts,
The aroma plays, a song of beasts.
A whiff of spice, or bread's warm rise,
Brings forth connections, a sweet surprise.

With every bite, a tale unfolds,
Of mem'ries shared, of love that molds.
In every crumb, the past awakes,
In savory dreams, our heart retakes.

Like laughter soft, or whispers near,
These scents surround us, ever dear.
Through seasons change and moments live,
The flavors blend, the heart will give.

Around the table, souls unite,
With every meal, the world feels right.
In foods we share, our spirits climb,
The aroma lingers, a love in rhyme.

Harvesting Honesty

In fields of truth, we sow the seeds,
With honesty sprouting, fulfilling needs.
Each word we share, a gentle grace,
Unraveling doubt in this safe space.

Through murmurs soft and glances bright,
We cultivate trust, hearts take flight.
With every story, layers reveal,
In peeling back, our fears we heal.

With roots so deep, we hold the ground,
In honest moments, pure love found.
Though storms may come, and shadows play,
Together we stand, come what may.

Fruits of our labor, bright and sweet,
In every truth, our souls complete.
We gather knowledge, wisdom's glow,
In honesty's embrace, we grow.

So let us harvest, hand in hand,
The trust we build, a sacred land.
In every heart, let truth abide,
With honesty, let love reside.

like Stars Entwined

In velvet skies, where dreams collide,
We dance like stars, with love as guide.
Each moment glows, with whispers bright,
An endless journey, hearts take flight.

With cosmic grace, we weave our paths,
In constellations, shared heart laughs.
Through cosmic storms and tranquil nights,
Our orbits blend, with twinkling lights.

In shadows cast, we still shine clear,
Connected souls, forever near.
Through time and space, we find our place,
A galaxy of love's embrace.

When worlds apart, still we ignite,
With secret wishes that feel so right.
Like constellations, drawn so fine,
In endless realms, our hearts align.

So let the universe sing our song,
As stars entwined, where we belong.
In every wish upon the night,
We write our story, bold and bright.

Shadows that Shine

In the dusk's gentle touch,
Shadows dance on the ground,
Echoes of whispers linger,
In silence, grace is found.

Flickers of light play softly,
Embracing the night's cool breath,
In the shadows, dreams awaken,
Life and magic entwined in depth.

Stars peek through the branches,
Guiding with their distant glow,
Every flicker tells a story,
Of paths we long to know.

Hold tight to the fleeting moments,
When darkness brings the light,
In shadows that softly shimmer,
Hope ignites the night.

For in every breath of twilight,
Lies a promise yet to bloom,
In shadows that shine through ages,
We weave a vibrant room.

Bonds Beyond Time

Threads of laughter and whispers,
Weaving through hearts like gold,
Time may change our faces,
But never will we fold.

In the tapestry of moments,
Memories shimmer bright,
Bonds that stretch through the ages,
Hold us close in the night.

Every touch, every heartbeat,
An echo of love divine,
Through the storms and the stillness,
Our souls forever entwine.

With each new dawn unfolding,
A chapter yet to explore,
Together we build our stories,
With bonds that ever soar.

Beyond the hands of the clock,
In unity, we shall climb,
For love knows no beginning,
Only bonds beyond time.

Laughter Under the Stars

In the hush of evening's grace,
Laughter rings through the trees,
Underneath the starry sky,
A symphony in the breeze.

Each twinkle holds a secret,
Whispered soft by the night,
We share our dreams and wishes,
In pure, unfiltered light.

With every chuckle and giggle,
The cosmos joins the play,
Dancing in the silence,
As shadows fade away.

Fires crackle with stories,
Our hearts open wide,
In laughter's sweet embrace,
Together, we abide.

Beneath celestial wonders,
In unity we find,
The joy in simple moments,
Laughter, love intertwined.

Hearts That Understand

In a world that spins so fast,
There lies a gentle grace,
Hearts that recognize the truth,
In every kind embrace.

Words may falter and fade,
But feelings always stay,
In silence, we connect deeply,
Finding a brighter way.

Through storms and through sunshine,
Together we shall stand,
Guided by compassion,
In hearts that understand.

In the fabric of our journey,
Love is the golden thread,
We sketch our dreams in kindness,
With every word unsaid.

So let us wander onward,
Hand in heart, we're a brand,
In this sacred dance of life,
With hearts that understand.

A Safe Haven

In the quiet of the night, we find,
A place where worries fade away.
The warmth of hearts forever kind,
In this safe haven, here we stay.

Whispers of love, softly soar,
As dreams take flight on silver wings.
Together we face what lies in store,
In our haven, peace it brings.

Through storms that rage and darkened skies,
We shelter here, we won't be lost.
With every tear and every sigh,
Love's embrace will bear the cost.

The world outside may storm and cry,
But in our hearts, the sun will shine.
Together we'll learn how to fly,
In this haven, forever thine.

So hand in hand, we'll light the way,
Through every trial, every test.
Our safe haven is here to stay,
In love and faith, we find our rest.

Footprints in the Sand

Along the shore where waves caress,
Footprints linger, memories made.
Each step a story to confess,
In the sand, our dreams displayed.

As tides may shift and seasons change,
Those marks tell tales of days gone by.
In each imprint, nothing strange,
A journey shared beneath the sky.

Sunset glows, the world turns gold,
Stories whispered in the breeze.
The warmth of days, in dreams retold,
Footprints fade, yet love won't cease.

Through the storms, our paths remain,
Dancing lightly on shifting ground.
Trails of laughter, echoes of pain,
In golden grains, our hopes are found.

So let the waves wash over me,
And let the sand bear all we've planned.
With every step, together we'll be,
Writing love's tale in footprints in the sand.

Guiding Lights

In the darkness, stars ignite,
A tapestry of dreams above.
Each glimmer shines, a guiding light,
And fills the heart with hope and love.

Through the shadows, we find our way,
As every step brings us near.
With every dawn, a new display,
Our guiding lights will chase the fear.

Together, hand in hand we'll walk,
The path ahead may twist and turn.
With every whispered, gentle talk,
Our guiding lights will always burn.

In moments lost, we won't despair,
For constellations lead us home.
With open hearts, our burdens bear,
In guiding lights, we'll never roam.

So confide in dreams, let courage rise,
Illuminate the road ahead.
With every star that fills the skies,
Our guiding lights will never fade.

Holding Hands Through Storms

When thunder rolls and shadows fall,
We stand together, hearts held tight.
In every trial, we hear the call,
Holding hands, we face the night.

Through winds that howl and rain that pours,
We will not falter, we will not break.
With every step, our spirit soars,
In unity, we'll never shake.

The tempest rages, but love's embrace,
Can anchor souls and calm the fears.
Through every challenge, we find our place,
Holding hands, we'll dry the tears.

In the chaos, our hearts align,
As lightning strikes with fearsome grace.
Together, love, forever divine,
Through storms we stride, we'll find our space.

So when the skies darken above,
Know that our bond will see us through.
Holding hands, we conquer with love,
Through every storm, it's me and you.

The Compass of Kinship

In the quiet of evening glow,
We gather, hands entwined,
Stories woven in whispers,
Love's light forever enshrined.

Through laughter and through tears,
We navigate the storms,
Hearts aligned in unity,
A bond that keeps us warm.

Time may test our tethered ties,
Yet strong we stand, undaunted,
With every sunset we embrace,
A future brightly haunted.

In every shared adventure,
Our spirits dance like flames,
We write our destiny,
In kinship, we are named.

Together, we break the silence,
Through memories, we find,
The compass of our journey,
In love, our hearts aligned.

Souls Intertwined

In the tapestry of night,
Our laughter's gentle thread,
With each whisper, a spark,
Every promise softly said.

You are the moon's embrace,
In shadows, we can shine,
Two souls in perfect rhythm,
A melody divine.

Through valleys deep and wide,
We tread with steadfast feet,
In every step together,
Our journey feels complete.

Mirrors of reflections,
In each other's gaze we find,
A universe unfolding,
Two hearts, forever twined.

Hand in hand, we wander,
With each breath, love's design,
In the story of existence,
Our souls will ever shine.

When Laughter Echoes

Beneath the golden sun,
We gather, hearts aglow,
Every jest and tale woven,
In the warmth of laughter's flow.

The echoes dance like sunlight,
In every heartfelt cheer,
Moments cherished in our minds,
Memories we hold dear.

Let the world fade away,
As joy becomes our song,
In the rhythm of our laughter,
Together, we belong.

The simple joys unite us,
In the storm, we stand tall,
When laughter echoes brightly,
We rise above it all.

In every chuckle shared,
In every joyful tear,
When laughter echoes freely,
Our hearts have nothing to fear.

The Haven of Heartbeats

In the stillness of the night,
Where shadows softly play,
I find you, my refuge,
In the warmth of love's sway.

Amidst life's endless chaos,
Your heartbeat is my song,
A melody of safety,
Where I know I belong.

Together in this haven,
We weave our dreams anew,
In whispers of tomorrow,
All that I need is you.

Through each pulse, connection,
Our spirits gently soar,
In the haven of heartbeats,
I'll love you evermore.

So let the world keep turning,
With you, I face the fight,
In the haven of heartbeats,
I find my endless light.

One Heart, Many Paths

In the garden of choices, we stand,
Wandering through dreams hand in hand.
Each step we take, a thread we weave,
With compassion's touch, we dare to believe.

Winding roads beneath the sky,
Whispers of hope will never die.
United in spirit, we forge ahead,
One heart guiding where others have tread.

Journeys diverge, yet still we meet,
In every stranger, a story sweet.
With open minds, we greet the day,
A tapestry woven in the light of play.

Though paths may twist and often turn,
In the depths of love, we always yearn.
Together we learn, together we grow,
In the dance of peace, our spirits flow.

So fear not the journey, embrace the quest,
For each path taken reveals our best.
In one heart's rhythm, many trails sing,
Harmony echoes in everything.

Seeds of Kindness

Tiny seeds scattered wide,
Grow in the wild, where hearts abide.
With gentle hands, we plant the care,
In steadfast soil, kindness we share.

A smile's warmth warms the cold,
Simple acts of love unfold.
With every gesture, we sow a spark,
Lighting the way through shadows dark.

In the laughter of children playing,
In the comfort of words, gently saying.
A helping hand, a listening ear,
We nurture bonds that draw us near.

As seasons shift and times will change,
The roots of kindness, they rearrange.
From little sprouts, great trees will rise,
Reaching for hope in boundless skies.

So let us sow in every heart,
A garden of love, a work of art.
With seeds of kindness, let us create,
A world united, a hopeful state.

The Light Within Shadows

In the depths where shadows play,
A flicker of light guides the way.
In whispered fears and silent cries,
Hope's gentle glow shall never die.

Hidden truths await the dawn,
Beneath the weight, we carry on.
Through trials faced, we learn to see,
The strength within our destiny.

Every dream, a spark ignites,
Illuminating darkest nights.
With courage born from scars we've known,
We find the light that's truly our own.

In fleeting moments, grace appears,
Turning sorrow into cheers.
As we embrace both dark and bright,
We navigate the dance of light.

So hold the flame, let spirits rise,
In unity, we claim our prize.
For within shadows, love will find,
The radiant truth of heart and mind.

Rituals of Remembrance

In gentle whispers of the past,
We honor moments meant to last.
With open hearts, we gather near,
To celebrate, to shed a tear.

Each story shared, a thread we spin,
Connecting lives, where we have been.
In sacred space, our memories weave,
A tapestry of love, we believe.

From candlelight to spoken word,
In silence felt, and echoes heard.
We carry forth those who have gone,
In every heartbeat, their spirit's song.

As seasons change and time decays,
We hold them close in myriad ways.
Through rituals soft and days adorned,
Their light within us, forever warmed.

So let us gather, lift the veil,
Embrace the past where love prevails.
In remembrance, may we find our voice,
In shared remembrance, we rejoice.

The Comfort of Companionship

In times of joy, in times of strife,
We share our dreams and hold our hands.
Through laughter's light and sorrow's knife,
Together we forge our steadfast plans.

With whispers soft and smiles so bright,
Our spirits soar, like birds in flight.
In silence shared, in deep delight,
The warmth of love ignites the night.

Through fleeting days and endless nights,
Each moment glows, a cherished thread.
We navigate the highest heights,
With hearts entwined, where souls are fed.

No burden borne is ours alone,
In shadows cast, we shine out bold.
In every stone, our love has grown,
A tapestry of joy unrolled.

So here we stand, side by side,
With memories rich, our laughter rings.
In life's vast dance, a boundless tide,
We find our strength in simple things.

Tides of Affection

The ocean pulls and gently gives,
Its waves embrace the sandy shore.
Like tides of love, our spirit lives,
In every crash, we crave for more.

As moonlight dances on the sea,
Your hand in mine, so warm, so near.
The whispered breeze sets our hearts free,
In every wave, our truth is clear.

Beneath the stars, our dreams take flight,
The currents shift, yet stay the same.
With each sunrise that ends the night,
We find the spark that fuels our flame.

Through changing tides, we stand our ground,
With every ebb, a trust restored.
In every heart, our love is found,
A sacred bond we can't afford.

So as we drift on life's wide stream,
With faith as our unfailing guide,
Let's chase the waves, fulfill our dream,
With tides of love that never hide.

The Unseen Embrace

In quiet corners of the mind,
Where thoughts take shape and softly weave,
An unseen bond, a love so kind,
Whispers of trust that we believe.

When shadows fall, you seem so near,
A comforting light that guides my way.
In laughter shared, in every tear,
Your essence blooms like flowers in May.

Through stormy nights and calmest skies,
Your spirit dances in the air.
With every glance, our hearts arise,
A tapestry of love laid bare.

We may not touch, yet feel the pull,
A force unseen that draws us close.
In every heartbeat, oh so full,
The unseen embrace, we cherish most.

So here we stand, though miles apart,
Connected by the threads of fate.
With every beat, you touch my heart,
In this embrace, we elevate.

Chasing Stars Together

Beneath a sky of endless night,
We chase the stars, our hopes align.
In dreams of wish and pure delight,
We journey forth, our hearts entwined.

With every spark that lights the dark,
A guiding flame, a beacon bright.
Through whispered dreams, we leave our mark,
In every twinkle, love takes flight.

Through cosmic seas, we sail so free,
With hands that clasp and eyes that gleam.
In every glance a galaxy,
Together, we create a dream.

As constellations map our course,
We chart the skies, our boundless quest.
With every pulse, a cosmic force,
In unity, we find our rest.

So let us roam the heavens wide,
With stardust hearts and souls ablaze.
In every moment, side by side,
We'll dance among the stars always.

Bonds Beyond Time

Across vast seas, our spirits soar,
In whispered winds, we seek for more.
Moments shared, a bridge we build,
In timeless echoes, hearts are filled.

In laughter's glow, we find our strength,
A tapestry woven, a boundless length.
With every dawn, our love takes flight,
Together we chase the fading light.

Memory's threads, entwined divine,
Through trials faced, our stars align.
Adventures shared, through thick and thin,
In every loss, we find our win.

Seasons change, yet we stand tall,
In every rise, we never fall.
The past and future, one single thread,
In bonds beyond time, our spirits wed.

Unmasking the Heart

Beneath the surface, secrets lie,
In tender moments, we learn to fly.
With each shared glance, our truths unfold,
In quiet corners, our stories told.

Unveiling shadows, fears take flight,
In candid whispers, we find the light.
The weight of silence begins to lift,
In vulnerability, we find our gift.

No more pretense, just raw and real,
In honest words, we begin to heal.
Each word a promise, each tear a sign,
In unmasking the heart, our souls entwine.

Through the storms and darkest nights,
Together we shine, our love ignites.
With every heartbeat, truth we embrace,
In unmasking the heart, we find our place.

Threads of Trust

In gentle hands, we weave a dream,
Each whispered promise, a silver beam.
Through trials faced, we stand as one,
In threads of trust, our battle's won.

Woven tightly, this bond so rare,
In storms and sun, we learn to share.
Through words unspoken, we understand,
In the fabric of love, we make our stand.

With honest hearts, we face the tide,
In every challenge, we choose to bide.
As shadows linger, our light will shine,
In threads of trust, our souls align.

Together we rise, never to fall,
In unity's strength, we conquer all.
A tapestry rich, a tale we write,
In threads of trust, our future's bright.

Companionship in Silence

In stillness shared, our hearts collide,
In sacred comfort, where secrets hide.
A glance exchanged speaks louder than words,
In companionship, our souls have stirred.

Through quiet moments, we find our grace,
In gentle pauses, we embrace space.
No need for noise, just presence felt,
In the silence, our fears melt.

The world around fades into a blur,
In calm camaraderie, we gently stir.
With every heartbeat, we write our song,
In companionship, we both belong.

In shared horizons, where dreams reside,
In the hush of nights, our hearts confide.
Beyond the words, our bond runs deep,
In companionship in silence, we leap.

The Comfort of Knowing

In quiet moments, peace surrounds,
A gentle whisper, soft and calm.
The heart finds solace in its sound,
A balm for wounds, a soothing balm.

In shadows cast by doubt and fear,
We find our strength, our guiding light.
A knowing presence always near,
Embracing us throughout the night.

With every step, we walk anew,
The path ahead is rich and bright.
In trust, we find our courage true,
And face the dawn with hope and might.

The comfort blooms in every heart,
A shared connection, warm and deep.
In unity, we play our part,
A sacred bond that we will keep.

So let us treasure what we know,
In every breath, in every sigh.
For in this life, love's seeds we sow,
And find our place beneath the sky.

Hearts Without Masks

Beneath the smiles, the shadows hide,
A longing gaze, a truth untold.
We strip away the false and pride,
And let our stories softly unfold.

In every glance, a world awaits,
The fearless truth behind the gaze.
We open wide our guarded gates,
Embracing love in all its ways.

To stand as one, both strong and vulnerable,
To dance in light without a shield.
In honesty, we find what's wonderful,
And in this truth, our fates are sealed.

So take my hand, let's walk this road,
No masks to hide, no fears to chase.
In purest hearts, our love bestowed,
We'll find our strength in each embrace.

Together, we will face the storm,
As nothing can our ties erase.
With hearts unmasked, we are reborn,
In love and truth, we find our place.

The Circle of Resonance

In gentle waves, the echoes rise,
A harmony of hearts and souls.
Each note a truth, a sweet surprise,
Together, we make music whole.

The circle grows, our voices blend,
A tapestry of dreams and hopes.
In every chord, we find a friend,
And lift each other as we cope.

As rhythms dance and pulses flow,
United in this sacred space.
In resonance, our spirits glow,
Reflecting love in every trace.

With every turn, the magic weaves,
A bond unbroken, ever strong.
In every heart, the spirit believes,
And finds its place where it belongs.

So let us sing, together loud,
In the embrace of unity.
For in this circle, we are proud,
Resonating, eternally.

Reflections in a Quiet Pond

Beneath the surface, still and deep,
The world above is mirrored clear.
In tranquil moments, secrets keep,
A silent space where thoughts adhere.

The trees, they bend, the breeze it sighs,
As ripples dance upon the face.
In mirrored depths, our spirit flies,
Finding peace in nature's grace.

Each whisper soft, each shadow cast,
Reveals the truths we hold inside.
In quiet waters, memories last,
And show us where our dreams reside.

So watch the pond, the skies above,
For in the stillness, wisdom lies.
In gentle waves, we find our love,
Reflecting hope beneath the skies.

As twilight falls, the stars align,
In quietude, our thoughts are drawn.
With every glance, a heart entwined,
In peacefulness, we greet the dawn.

The Language of the Heart

In whispers soft, the heart confides,
Emotions dance, like waves and tides.
A touch, a glance, speaks louder still,
A silent promise, a gentle thrill.

Each heartbeat plays a tender song,
Binding souls where they belong.
In rhythm sweet, love finds its way,
Uniting hearts, come what may.

Through laughter bright and tears that fall,
The language we share connects us all.
Unspoken words, their truths reveal,
In the depths of feeling, we learn to heal.

Time may change the paths we take,
But the heart's resolve will never break.
In every glance, yet unobserved,
Lies the strength of love, undeterred.

So listen close, let your heart lead,
Where kindness flows, and spirits feed.
Together in this sacred art,
We celebrate the language of the heart.

Leaving No One Behind

In crowded rooms, where shadows play,
Each person seeks to find their way.
A friendly hand, a smiling face,
Can turn despair into embrace.

We gather strength when we unite,
Through darkest hours, we spark the light.
No one should walk this path alone,
Together, we create our home.

With open hearts, we stand as one,
Through trials faced, we've just begun.
Empathy, our guiding star,
To lift each other near and far.

In every struggle, we'll prevail,
With voices strong, we lift the veil.
Hand in hand, we build a bridge,
To conquer doubt, to rise, and live.

Leaving no one, we strive to find,
The strength that lives in every kind.
Together, brighter futures gleam,
In love and hope, we weave our dream.

Kindred Vines

In gardens vast, our spirits twine,
Like kindred vines, interlaced, entwined.
Through seasons changed, we grow and bloom,
With roots so deep, we silence gloom.

In joy and sorrow, hand in hand,
We nurture dreams, like grains of sand.
Each petal falls, yet carries grace,
In every moment, find our place.

Through storms we sway but do not break,
Embracing love for each other's sake.
Unyielding trust, a firm embrace,
In this warm garden, we find our space.

With colors bright, our laughter rings,
Reflecting all the joy life brings.
Together we reach for the sun,
In the tapestry of love, we run.

As kindred vines, we stretch and grow,
In nature's song, our hearts will flow.
With every pulse, our spirits shine,
In life's rich soil, love is divine.

Gifts of the Spirit

Each dawn brings forth a brand new gift,
In gentle ways, our spirits lift.
A smile, a word, a hand to hold,
In every moment, love untold.

With kindness shared, the world can change,
Transforming hearts, it feels so strange.
Yet in the warmth of each embrace,
We find our true and rightful place.

Compassion flows like rivers wide,
Washing sorrows, turning the tide.
In every act, let mercy bloom,
Dispelling shadows, making room.

Gratitude, a powerful thread,
Weaving connections where we tread.
In grateful hearts, we see the light,
Illuminating paths so bright.

So let us share these gifts we bear,
In every moment, everywhere.
Together, let our spirits sing,
In love's embrace, we find our wings.

Echoes of Loyalty

In shadows cast by fervent hearts,
A promise made, never departs.
Through storms we tread, hand in hand,
A bond unbroken, forever we'll stand.

Voices of trust in the calm night air,
Each word a thread, a testament rare.
Through trials faced, our spirits ignite,
Bound by loyalty, shining so bright.

Echoes resound in the quiet space,
In each other's eyes, we find our place.
Through thick and thin, our paths align,
In this sacred bond, our hearts entwine.

With every challenge, our strength will grow,
The seeds of loyalty, we endlessly sow.
Hand in hand, come what may,
Together we'll chase the dawn of day.

So let the echoes of loyalty ring,
In the tapestry of life, we cling.
For through the years, come joy or strife,
In loyalty's arms, we find our life.

The Language of Understanding

In silence shared, we speak so clear,
A whispered truth, drawing near.
With eyes that meet, worlds intertwine,
In this language, so divine.

Words unspoken, yet deeply felt,
In every glance, emotions melt.
A bridge of trust, we build so strong,
In this understanding, we belong.

From hearts that listen, wisdom flows,
In gentle gestures, love just grows.
Through storms of doubt, we hold the line,
In understanding, we brightly shine.

The rhythm of life, a dance so sweet,
In every heartbeat, our souls entreat.
As seasons change, our minds align,
In this language, so rare and fine.

So let us cherish this gentle grace,
In the warmth of love, we find our place.
Through open hearts, we'll always find,
The beautiful art of being kind.

Genuine Reflections

In mirrors clear, we search our soul,
Reflecting truths that make us whole.
With every flaw, a lesson learned,
In genuine light, our spirits burned.

The winds of change, they whisper soft,
Through trials faced, we rise aloft.
In every stumble, we find our grace,
Genuine reflections in time and space.

With every heartbeat, a story told,
In laughter shared, our warmth unfolds.
Through sunny days and shadows cast,
We gather moments, steadfast and vast.

In honesty's glow, we shed our pride,
In genuine love, we will abide.
For in this journey, hand in hand,
We find our truth, and together we stand.

So let reflections guide our way,
In every dawn of a brand new day.
With open hearts, let's walk in tune,
In genuine light, beneath the moon.

In the Garden of Kindred Spirits

Among the blooms, our laughter sings,
In the garden where friendship springs.
With every petal, a story shared,
In kindred hearts, we have cared.

The fragrance of trust fills the air,
In gentle breezes, we find our fare.
Together we plant, together we reap,
In this garden, our memories keep.

Through seasons that change, we stay aligned,
With roots entangled, our souls intertwined.
In every color, a bond so bright,
In the garden of spirits, our hearts take flight.

With each sunrise, new dreams arise,
In this sacred space, our spirits fly.
Among the ferns, beneath the trees,
In kindred spirits, we find our ease.

So let us wander, hand in hand,
In the garden where love has been planned.
For in this beauty, we find our truth,
In the garden of kindred spirits, eternal youth.

A Journey of Souls

Through the mist of time we tread,
Each step a whisper, softly said.
Carrying stories in our hearts,
A tapestry where life imparts.

Guided by stars that shine so bright,
Navigating through the night.
With every heartbeat, bonds are formed,
In unity, our spirits warmed.

Paths entwined like vines that climb,
In every laugh, a hope sublime.
Together we face the hills that rise,
Hand in hand under vast skies.

From shore to shore, we wander free,
A thousand dreams, a symphony.
In every tear, a tale unfolds,
Of journeys shared and truths retold.

So let us roam, our souls ignite,
In the dance of shadows and light.
For in this voyage, we find our role,
A journey everlasting, the soul's goal.

The Essence of Belonging

In the heart's embrace, we find our place,
A gentle pull, a warm trace.
Fingers intertwined, we stand tall,
Echoes of laughter, a cherished call.

With every glance, a world unfolds,
In quiet moments, a love behold.
Roots as deep as the ancient trees,
Together we sway with the evening breeze.

Through storms we walk, unafraid,
In the shadows, our fears laid.
An unspoken bond, strong and true,
In the tapestry of me and you.

In communal fires, our stories glow,
Each voice a thread, a vibrant flow.
From shared dreams to silent songs,
In this essence, we all belong.

In the fabric of life, we weave,
A shared heartbeat that we believe.
Forever together, through dusk and dawn,
In this essence, we are never alone.

A Flame that Guides

In the darkness, a flicker shines,
A beacon bright, where hope aligns.
Through trials faced and paths unknown,
This flame ignites the spirit's throne.

With every laugh and tear we share,
A warmth that lingers, deep and rare.
In shadows cast, we find our light,
Together we blaze, dispelling night.

Upon this path, the fire glows,
Leading us where the wild wind blows.
With every step, our courage grows,
In this dance of life, we compose.

Through storms and trials, we stay bold,
With hands united, stories told.
In every heart, this flame resides,
A guiding force where love abides.

So let it burn, both fierce and bright,
A testament of strength and might.
For in this warmth, our spirits soar,
A flame that guides, forevermore.

The Strength of Togetherness

In unity, we find our power,
Together we bloom like a vibrant flower.
Each voice a note in a grand refrain,
Creating strength from joy and pain.

Shoulder to shoulder, we face the tide,
In the warmth of love, we confide.
Hand in hand, we rise anew,
In this gathering, dreams come true.

Through whispers soft and laughter loud,
We stand as one, unbowed, unbowed.
In the heart of the storm, we remain,
Bound by a bond no force can strain.

With courage steeped in shared embrace,
We carve our path, we find our space.
Together we weather, shine, and grow,
In the garden where hope's seeds sow.

So let us cherish this sacred bond,
A sanctuary where we respond.
For in togetherness, we find our way,
The strength that guides us, come what may.

The Golden Circle

In the heart of the land, they stand so bright,
A circle of warmth, from morning to night.
Each ray a promise, a story unveiled,
In unity's glow, all hardship curtailed.

Around the fire, laughter and cheer,
Two souls entwined, their dreams appear.
Together they shine, like stars in the sky,
In the golden circle, time passes by.

With hands intertwined, they journey afar,
Guided by hope, like a steadfast star.
Through seasons of change, their bond will remain,
In the golden circle, love's sweet refrain.

The whispers of nature, in the breeze they hear,
Echoing softly, drawing them near.
In the still of the night, by the moon's gentle light,
Their hearts dance together, pure and so bright.

Together they dance, in harmony's tune,
Under the gaze of the watchful moon.
In the warmth of their circle, they thrive and they grow,
In the golden embrace, life's blessings bestow.

Silent Support

In shadows they stand, with hearts so true,
Offering strength in all that we do.
With words unspoken, they lend us their grace,
In every challenge, they find their place.

A gentle embrace, when the days feel long,
With actions that echo a silent song.
Under the surface, their spirits ignite,
A bond unbreakable, a guiding light.

Through struggles and storms, they anchor our souls,
In moments of doubt, they make us feel whole.
When words are too heavy, their presence can mend,
In the silence of love, our spirits ascend.

Together we rise, on the wings of support,
Building a fortress of love, our report.
In laughter and tears, we share the embrace,
In silence, we flourish, in love we find grace.

With every heartbeat, our strength intertwines,
In the quietest moments, our spirit aligns.
Through trials and triumphs, together we stand,
In silent support, united we band.

Reflections in the Mirror

In the glass we see, a story unfold,
Fragments of moments, both timid and bold.
Each smile a piece, of the journey we trace,
Reflections of life, time's tender embrace.

Glances of laughter, shadows of fears,
Memories captured, like a river of tears.
In stillness we ponder, what lies within,
The mirror reveals where we've been and we've sinned.

With every glance towards the shimmer so bright,
We find our true selves, hidden from sight.
In the realm of reflection, we learn to forgive,
To cherish the lessons, as long as we live.

Each wrinkle a story, each mark a refrain,
A tapestry woven of joy and of pain.
We embrace our full selves, in every embrace,
Finding beauty in all, every line has its place.

And as we look deeper, we may even find,
The love that resides, inside every mind.
In reflections of selves, we discover our worth,
In the mirror of life, we find our rebirth.

The Color of Nurture

In gardens of love, where soft petals bloom,
Colors of nurture dispel all the gloom.
Through tender touches, in whispers so sweet,
Compassion and kindness make each heart complete.

The warmth of a hug, in the midst of the storm,
An embrace with the sun, where all souls transform.
With patience and care, seeds of hope we sow,
In the color of nurture, love's beauty will grow.

Through struggles and trials, we shelter our dreams,
With colors of joy, and collective themes.
In laughter and solace, we cherish the spark,
With care in our hearts, we light up the dark.

In the palette of life, every hue holds a weight,
Moments of nurture, we gather and create.
Through storms of despair, we rise and we mend,
In the color of nurture, we find life's true friend.

A tapestry woven in shades of the heart,
Each layer a story, each stitch a new start.
With colors of nurture, we paint all around,
In the garden of life, love and hope can be found.

Weaving Together Stories

In threads of gold and dreams we weave,
Tales of joy, of loss, of love to believe.
Each stitch a moment, each knot a vow,
Binding our souls in the here and the how.

The fabric of life, so rich and so bright,
Holds whispers of hope in the hush of night.
Together we gather, with laughter and tears,
Weaving our stories throughout the years.

From distant places, our voices unite,
In harmony's melody, pure and light.
Through the tapestry varied, our spirits hold tight,
Creating connections that shine ever bright.

In every detail, a life left its trace,
Eras entwined in a warm embrace.
Each memory dances, each shadow sings,
A quilt of our journeys, the joy that it brings.

So let us remember, as we gather round,
The stories that shape us are beautifully bound.
In the loom of our hearts, let love be the thread,
For together we rise, far greater instead.

The Lighthouse in the Fog

Through swirling mist, a beacon stands tall,
Guiding lost sailors who heed its soft call.
With a flickering light cutting through the gray,
It whispers of safety, shows them the way.

Waves crash in fury, yet steadfast it beams,
A symbol of hope in the harshness of dreams.
For who in the darkness can bear all alone?
The lighthouse stands ready, its heart like a stone.

With each gentle pulse, it shares its warm glow,
Rising from shadows where few dare to go.
In storms of uncertainty, it shouts with might,
A promise unbroken, the dawn's welcome light.

So let us remember, when clouds cluster near,
The solace that comes when our vision seems unclear.
For in our own journeys, through fog thick and deep,
We find our own lighthouses, our secrets to keep.

To all weary travelers who search for the shore,
Fear not the dark waters, there's so much in store.
For though oft surrounded, in chaos and strife,
We'll always find lighthouses to guide through our life.

Anchored Souls

In the ocean's embrace, our spirits convene,
Two anchored souls in a world unforeseen.
With waves crashing close, we ride every tide,
Together, unyielding, we stand side by side.

The storms may be fierce, but our bond is the sail,
Through skies blue and gray, we'll never derail.
In harbors of silence, we whisper our dreams,
Entwined in the moonlight, we chart our regimes.

Through laughter and tears, we weather the years,
Navigating life's path with hopes and with fears.
In the depths of the sea, our love serves as a guide,
A compass unbroken, where trust can reside.

In calm and in chaos, we cultivate peace,
With every horizon, our hearts find release.
For in this vast ocean, our spirits will thrive,
Anchored together, we uniquely survive.

So sail through the waters, my dear, ever bold,
In the grand tale of life, watch our story unfold.
For anchored souls journey, together we'll roam,
Creating a haven, forever our home.

Embracing Imperfections

In the cracks of our hearts, beauty finds space,
In every small flaw, there's a warm, loving grace.
With gentle acceptance, our stories unfold,
Embracing the shadows, in gold they are told.

For no one is perfect, we each bear our scars,
Yet in our slight missteps, we shine like the stars.
A tapestry woven with threads not so straight,
We find in our journeys the warmth of our fate.

Through stumbles and fumbles, we learn to embrace,
The essence of living, this intricate chase.
In every misgiving, there's a lesson we find,
To celebrate life, with its twists and its binds.

So let us be kind, both to others and selves,
For each of us carries our stories like shelves.
A sanctuary crafted from laughter and tears,
With imperfections embraced, we'll conquer our fears.

In the rhythm of life, our hearts find their song,
With imperfections celebrated, we all belong.
For it's in our flaws that our true strength unfolds,
Embracing our journey, a tale to be told.

The Bridge of Sincerity

In whispers soft, the truth unfolds,
A path where hearts connect like gold.
With every step, the trust we find,
A bridge of words, sincere and kind.

In storms of doubt, we stand our ground,
With open hearts, true love is found.
Let honesty be our sturdy frame,
In this bright light, we fan the flame.

The laughter shared, the tears we shed,
These moments weave the life we've led.
Through trials faced, we grow and learn,
Together on this bridge, we yearn.

Each promise made, a solid stone,
In unity, we're never alone.
With every word, a bond we seal,
On this grand bridge, our souls reveal.

As seasons change, our roots grow deep,
In sincerity, our hearts will leap.
With every step, we forge our way,
On the bridge of truth, forever stay.

Harmonious Journeys

On winding paths where dreams take flight,
We seek the dawn, embrace the light.
With every step, our spirits soar,
In harmony, we ever explore.

Through valleys low and mountains high,
We share our hopes, we touch the sky.
In laughter's echo, we find our song,
Together, right where we belong.

Each challenge faced, a lesson learned,
In unity, our passion burned.
With every heartbeat, we align,
On journeys vast, our souls entwine.

With open hearts, we take the leap,
In every moment, our love we keep.
The world unfolds, a canvas wide,
In harmonious dance, we take our stride.

As stars above begin to gleam,
We navigate through every dream.
With trust as our guiding star,
We journey far, we journey far.

The Luminescent Bond

In shadows cast, we find the glow,
A bond so bright, it starts to flow.
With each soft touch, our warmth ignites,
Together, we illuminate the nights.

Through trials faced, we stand as one,
In every setback, we've just begun.
With laughter shared, our spirits rise,
In this embrace, our love defies.

The whispers blend in harmony,
Creating waves of ecstasy.
In quiet moments, we align,
A luminescent bond divine.

With every heartbeat, we create,
A dance of souls that can't abate.
In love's embrace, forever shine,
Together, hearts and spirits entwine.

As stars reflect our timeless grace,
In this bright glow, we find our place.
With every breath, our legacy,
A bond that glows for all to see.

Beyond the Surface

In oceans deep, where secrets lie,
We delve beneath, where dreams can fly.
With open hearts, we seek to know,
The depths within, the undertow.

Beneath the waves, the treasures gleam,
In currents strong, we ride the stream.
Each layer peels, a story told,
In hidden depths, our spirits bold.

Through murky waters, truth will show,
In honesty, our hearts will grow.
As we explore, hand in hand,
Together, we're a steadfast band.

In tranquil depths, we find our peace,
Where doubts dissolve, and fears release.
With every dive, we rise anew,
Beyond the surface, ours is true.

In whispered dreams, our souls connect,
A journey rich with pure respect.
For in the depths, our love is pure,
Beyond the surface, we are sure.

Underneath the Surface

Beneath the calm, the currents flow,
Whispers of secrets, hidden below.
Ripples of stories, softly they weave,
In depths of silence, we learn to believe.

The weight of shadows, the dance of dreams,
Echoes of laughter, or so it seems.
Bubbles of thoughts, they rise and fall,
In the quiet water, they speak to us all.

Tides of emotions, all ebb and flow,
Carried away, where few dare to go.
Each wave a heartbeat, each splash a sigh,
A world uncharted, that whispers goodbye.

The journey inward, a quest for light,
Navigating darkness, with all of our might.
And in the stillness, we start to see,
The beauty of truths that set us free.

So plunge in deep, where the wildness stirs,
Embrace the silence, feel the soft whirs.
For underneath the surface, we find our way,
In the depths of our heart, come what may.

The Art of Being Seen

In crowded rooms, we wear our masks,
Hiding our hopes, in silence it basks.
A smile may shine, but eyes tell the tale,
Of unspoken stories, and dreams that prevails.

To truly be seen, is a delicate dance,
A moment of courage, given the chance.
The vulnerability, it cuts like a knife,
Yet in that exposure, we discover life.

Through tender glances, connections ignite,
The warmth of the heart, in the depths of the night.
We lean in closer, our fears we release,
In the art of being seen, we find our peace.

So speak your truth, let your colors show,
For in every heartbeat, there's magic to know.
Embrace the boldness, stand firm in your skin,
In the art of being seen, we truly begin.

Together we shine, like stars in the skies,
Illuminating paths, cutting through lies.
For when we are seen, we unite as one,
In the beauty of living, we have just begun.

Shadows and Light

In the corner, shadows dwell,
Softly they whisper, a secret to tell.
Light flickers bravely, in every crevice,
Dancing with darkness, a timeless premise.

The contrast of worlds, both warm and cold,
Tales of the silent, the brave and the bold.
With each breath taken, a balance we chase,
In shadows and light, we find our place.

Illuminated dreams, that fade into dusk,
Whispers of hope, in shadows we trust.
The chiaroscuro, both tender and fierce,
Holds within its grasp, our hearts it can pierce.

As light meets the shadow, they dance, they sway,
Crafting our stories, come what may.
For every darkness, a flicker will glow,
In shadows and light, our truths we will show.

So dwell in the balance, embrace the unknown,
In shadows and light, we're never alone.
For each holds a part, in the tapestry fine,
Woven together, forever they shine.

Unwavering Unison

In the stillness, our souls align,
A harmony crafted, in rhythm divine.
With hearts intertwined, we beat as one,
Facing the storms, till the new day's begun.

In moments of silence, our voices entwine,
A chorus of strength, with each subtle sign.
Together we stand, through thick and thin,
In unwavering unison, we find our spin.

The laughter we share, a melody sweet,
In the dance of our story, we find our beat.
Resilient as rivers, we flow side by side,
In unwavering unison, with nothing to hide.

Through trials and triumphs, we rise above,
An orchestra playing, the song of our love.
Each note unique, yet blended just right,
In the harmony found, we shine ever bright.

So lift up your voice, let your spirit soar,
For in this connection, we're bound to explore.
An infinite journey, through life's tangled run,
In unwavering unison, we've already won.

Unspoken Promises

In the silence, words remain,
Whispers of hope dance like rain.
Hearts in shadows know the truth,
Unveiling dreams of gentle youth.

Fingers brush, igniting flames,
Unseen vows without the names.
Promises linger in the air,
Silent echoes of tender care.

In the twilight's soft embrace,
Time stands still in this shared space.
Our eyes speak the tales untold,
A love that's fierce, yet soft and bold.

When the world fades from our view,
We find strength in bonds so true.
Though unvoiced, our hearts align,
In the depths, your soul is mine.

Through the storms and darkest nights,
Together we'll find our own lights.
For in the quiet, trust we weave,
In unspoken dreams, we believe.

The Dance of Kindred Spirits

In twilight glow, our spirits soar,
Two hearts as one, forevermore.
With each step, the cosmos sings,
A harmony that true love brings.

We twirl beneath the starry skies,
In every glance, a thousand sighs.
Wrapped in music, our souls entwined,
An endless dance, beautifully timed.

Time stands still, the world fades away,
In this moment, forever we stay.
Laughter echoes through the night,
In this rhythm, everything feels right.

Hand in hand, we chase the light,
With every spin, we ignite the night.
Together we leap, we glide, we flow,
A tapestry of joy we sow.

In each heartbeat, a vibrant beat,
Kindred spirits, our souls complete.
Through the dance, our love shines bright,
Guided by the moon's soft light.

A Tapestry of Souls

Threads of fate, entwined we stand,
Woven tightly, a vibrant strand.
In the fabric of dreams we share,
A masterpiece beyond compare.

Colors blend in perfect hues,
Every shade tells a tale that's true.
In laughter and tears, we find our way,
An intricate dance in life's ballet.

Stitches of joy and sorrow sew,
Crafting bonds that ever grow.
Paths once separate now align,
In this tapestry, our lives entwine.

Through storms and sunshine, we create,
A tapestry that cannot wait.
Each moment cherished, woven tight,
A living canvas, a pure delight.

In the end, when the threads unwind,
A legacy of love we'll find.
For in each soul, a story told,
A tapestry rich, a treasure gold.

Radiant Connections

In the glow of the morning sun,
Our hearts awaken, two become one.
With every smile, a spark ignites,
Lighting up the darkest nights.

Eyes that shimmer with a knowing glance,
In silent rhythms, we weave our dance.
Through whispered dreams and tender ties,
We find our strength in each other's sighs.

In this world of chaos, we remain,
Anchors of hope in joy and pain.
As stars align in perfect spheres,
We build our love through laughter and tears.

With every heartbeat, connections grow,
Radiant pathways, aglow with flow.
Together we rise, together we stand,
Crafting a future, hand in hand.

In the tapestry of souls entwined,
A symphony where love is blind.
With every moment, brilliantly bright,
Our radiant connections take flight.

In the Embrace of the Unseen

In shadows deep where whispers roam,
The unseen binds us, roots our home.
Through silent sighs and gentle dreams,
We dance beneath the moon's soft beams.

A touch that lingers, soft yet bold,
Stories shared, yet never told.
In quiet moments, hearts align,
We find the space where souls entwine.

Invisible ties that gently flow,
In laughter shared, in grief, we grow.
'Tis in the hush our truths unite,
In love's embrace, we find our light.

Through veils of time, we are drawn near,
In every pulse, we hold what's dear.
Though unseen paths we walk each day,
We cherish every step along the way.

So when the world feels cold and stark,
Remember love's warm, glowing spark.
In every silence, every glance,
We live in unity, life's sweet dance.

Heartstrings in Harmony

In whispers soft, our hearts take flight,
Playing melodies, pure delight.
Each note we share, a timeless art,
Together strung, two beating hearts.

The rhythm flows, a gentle tide,
With every beat, we walk side by side.
Through notes of joy and chords of pain,
We find the strength to rise again.

In twilight's glow, our song resounds,
In every silence, love confounds.
With fingers crossed, we weave a thread,
A symphony where all is said.

Resonance deep as ocean's wave,
In harmony, we learn to brave.
Together forged in trials faced,
In the heart's embrace, we're interlaced.

So let the music ever soar,
Through storms and calm, we'll seek the shore.
A dance of souls in perfect blend,
In heartstrings' grasp, we will transcend.

The Invisible Thread

A thread unseen that binds us tight,
In darkest hours, it brings the light.
Through tangled paths, we find our way,
In every word, together we stay.

Like morning dew on blades of grass,
Our moments shine, no need to pass.
In laughter shared, in tears that flow,
This invisible thread, we come to know.

With every heartbeat, a gentle pull,
In dreams we chase, our hearts are full.
Through trials faced, we're never apart,
This sacred thread connects each heart.

So when the winds begin to howl,
In fierce embrace, we know our vow.
No distance great can break or sever,
For in this bond, we are forever.

Let time unfold the tapestry,
Of every moment, you and me.
In the quiet spaces, we will find,
The invisible thread that shall bind.

Walking Beside Each Other

Two souls embark on paths anew,
With every step, the world feels true.
Through sunlit days and starry nights,
We walk together, hearts in flight.

In every laughter, in every tear,
We find our strength, we face our fear.
No road too long, no hill too steep,
Hand in hand, together we leap.

The journey's sweet, the moments vast,
In shadows cast, our love holds fast.
Through tangled woods and rivers wide,
With you beside me, I will abide.

Each turn we take, a chance to grow,
In every struggle, together we flow.
For in your eyes, I see my way,
As we walk beside each other each day.

So let the years unfold like pages,
In this book of love, through all the stages.
With every heartbeat, our stories blend,
Walking beside each other, till the end.

The Rhythm of Reliability

In daily whispers, a promise made,
The clock ticks steady, never delayed.
Hands that hold, plans that align,
A friend in shadows, both yours and mine.

Through storms and sun, the dance goes on,
A heart in sync, from dusk till dawn.
Trust like a river, flowing so deep,
In silence and laughter, memories we keep.

A shelter found in the storm's embrace,
In times of doubt, amidst the race.
Concrete walls, but warm inside,
With every heartbeat, we choose to abide.

No moment wasted, each breath we take,
In certainty born, the ground we stake.
Together we walk, hand in hand,
In the rhythm of life, we make our stand.

Whispers through Time

Beneath the starlit sky we share,
Voices echo softly, threading the air.
Fleeting moments, like leaves in the breeze,
Stories unfold among ancient trees.

Each heartbeat a tale, each sigh a song,
Timelines twist, where we all belong.
With every glance, a universe spins,
In whispers of fate, we learn what begins.

The sun will rise to paint the day,
Still, in shadows, memories play.
Across the ages, we find the path,
Connecting the past with gentle math.

Hold tight to the echoes, for they are gold,
In every whisper, wisdom unfolds.
Through the corridors of time we roam,
A tapestry woven, we call it home.

The Treasure of Authenticity

Beneath the surface, true gems lie,
Eagerly waiting, never too shy.
In a world of masks, so carefully worn,
The beauty of truth, in hearts reborn.

Colors and shapes, unique and rare,
Each voice a treasure, beyond compare.
Let go of the facade, let the light shine,
In the dance of realness, we intertwine.

With every flaw, a story untold,
In the warmth of acceptance, we find the bold.
Reveal your core, embrace the raw,
In the mirror of life, we see the law.

Simplicity whispers, joy comes alive,
In the arms of honesty, we truly thrive.
Together we stand, in this sacred space,
For authenticity is the warmest embrace.

Celestial Companions

Under the vastness of the night sky,
Stars twinkle softly, a cosmic sigh.
With every glance, a tethered spark,
In this silent dance, we leave our mark.

Planets align in a graceful waltz,
In constellations, our fate exalts.
Galaxies whisper the secrets untold,
A friendship woven in the folds of the bold.

From dusk till dawn, we rise and fall,
Together we journey, answering the call.
In this celestial realm, spirits collide,
Fellow travelers in time's endless ride.

With each heartbeat shared, we light the way,
In the universe vast, forever we stay.
Celestial companions, we sail the night,
In the embrace of the stars, we find our light.

The Ties That Free

In the whisper of winds, we find our song,
Threads of laughter binding us strong.
Through storms and sunshine, we gently sway,
With hearts that dance, we'll find our way.

In moments of silence, we've learned to speak,
In the warmth of connection, no need to seek.
Our souls entwined, they soar above,
Finding freedom in this bond of love.

Though paths may shift and seasons change,
The ties that bind, they never estrange.
In glances shared and stories told,
We weave a tapestry, rich and bold.

When shadows creep and doubts arise,
We hold each other, under endless skies.
For in this embrace, we rise anew,
The ties that free, they strengthen true.

So here we stand, side by side,
In unity's embrace, we abide.
With every heartbeat, our spirits soar,
The ties that free, forever more.

Heartstrings in Unison

In quiet moments, our hearts convene,
A melody played, soft and serene.
With every beat, a rhythm flows,
Heartstrings in unison, softly it grows.

Through trials faced and laughter shared,
A bond unbroken, love declared.
In vibrant colors, our dreams take flight,
Together we shine, a guiding light.

When fears arise and shadows loom,
Our hearts entwined, dispel the gloom.
Each note of hope, a sweet refrain,
In harmony's grasp, we feel no pain.

With gentle whispers, we make our way,
In dance of trust, we shall not sway.
For every heartbeat sings the truth,
Heartstrings in unison, eternal youth.

As twilight falls and stars appear,
In this vast world, we draw near.
Bound by a melody, sweet and sweet,
Heartstrings in unison, forever meet.

A Heartfelt Journey

With every step, a tale unfolds,
In the warmth of memories, life beholds.
Through paths we wander, hand in hand,
A heartfelt journey, we take our stand.

In valleys low and mountains high,
Our laughter echoes, a joyful cry.
Through trials faced, we find our stride,
In unity's strength, we shall abide.

With open hearts, we brave the new,
In every heartbeat, love shines through.
Creating moments, we cherish most,
In this heartfelt journey, we freely boast.

As seasons change and rivers flow,
With whispers soft, our feelings grow.
Together we travel, side by side,
A heartfelt journey, our hearts are wide.

In night's embrace, we dream and scheme,
While stars bear witness to every dream.
With gratitude deep, we walk this way,
A heartfelt journey, come what may.

Anchored in Understanding

In the depths of silence, we comprehend,
A tether woven, where hearts extend.
With compassion deep, we gently find,
Anchored in understanding, souls aligned.

Through storms of doubt and waves of fear,
We hold each other, forever near.
In every challenge, wisdom grows,
Anchored in understanding, love bestows.

With open minds, we share our dreams,
In vibrant hues, life's canvas gleams.
Together we navigate, side by side,
Anchored in understanding, we'll abide.

In moments shared, we come alive,
In laughter's echo, our spirits thrive.
A bridge of trust, unyielding and true,
Anchored in understanding, me and you.

So here's to the bond that holds us tight,
In darkest hours, you are my light.
With every heartbeat, we shall expand,
Anchored in understanding, hand in hand.

Threads of Compassion

In shadows deep, we find a spark,
A gentle hand to heal the dark.
With every touch, a story bent,
Threads of love, so close, so rent.

Through bitter storms and piercing cold,
We weave our dreams from courage bold.
Each thread a promise, soft and bright,
In the tapestry of shared light.

Compassion flows like rivers wide,
In every heart, let kindness bide.
We lift each other with our grace,
A warm embrace, a sacred space.

The world can change, a hand in hand,
With woven hearts, we take a stand.
In unity, we rise above,
Each thread a bond, a thread of love.

The Heart's Compass

In whispered winds, our hearts do steer,
Navigating paths both far and near.
With every beat, a guide unfolds,
A compass made of love, it holds.

When shadows fall, and doubts arise,
The heart's true north will crystallize.
Through storms and calm, we'll find our way,
With hope as light, we'll seize the day.

Each turn we take, a lesson learned,
In fires of change, our spirits burned.
With every mile, our courage grows,
The heart whispers what the spirit knows.

In stillness deep, we hear the call,
The compass guides through rise and fall.
With open hearts, the journey starts,
Together, bound, we'll play our parts.

Glimmers of Genuineness

In a world adorned with masks so bright,
Glimmers of truth shine through the night.
Authentic souls in silent grace,
Sharing warmth, a sacred space.

With gentle words, we break the mold,
In every glance, a story told.
The beauty lies in who we are,
As honest hearts, we raise the bar.

Through trials faced and shadows cast,
The light of genuineness holds fast.
In laughter shared and tears we weep,
A bond unbroken, strong and deep.

Each moment pure, a treasure rare,
In every gesture, love laid bare.
In hearts aligned, let kindness flow,
Together, in the truth, we grow.

The Fortress of Friendship

In storms that rage, a shelter stands,
A fortress built with loving hands.
In laughter shared and sorrows borne,
Friendship thrives, forever sworn.

Through trials faced and moments shared,
In every glance, we show we cared.
Each secret whispered, trust bestowed,
In unity, the heart's abode.

As seasons change, our roots grow deep,
In stories told, our promises keep.
With open arms, we greet the day,
Together strong, come what may.

Through every wound, we find the light,
In the fortress, love takes flight.
A bond unbreakable, true, and rare,
In friendship's heart, we know we care.

Printed in the USA
CPSIA information can be obtained
at www.ICGtesting.com
CBHW07094922112
17472CB00072B/29